THE LITTLE RAINDROP

Wendy Garrison Todd

THE LITTLE RAINDROP

Illustrated by
Sarah Zoutewelle-Morris

FINDHORN *Press*

First published by Findhorn Press in 2005

ISBN 1-84409-060-4

British Library Cataloguing-in-Publication Data.
A catalogue record for this book is available
from the British Library.

Edited by Kate Keogan
Cover design by Sarah-Zoutewelle-Morris and Thierry Bogliolo
Interior design by Thierry Bogliolo.

Printed and bound by WS Bookwell, Finland

Published by
Findhorn Press
305a The Park, Findhorn
Forres IV36 3TE
Scotland, UK
tel 01309 690582/fax 690036
info@findhornpress.com
www.findhornpress.com

This book is dedicated to my parents,
Hazel & Ron Garrison
who showed me the meaning of love.

The drop of water had no knowledge of anything before The Fall from the cloud. Nothing had been, until the moment when it had suddenly *winked* into existence, with an almost tangible wrench. In such incredible freedom, it had then experienced the exhilaration of freefall and, although it tried and tried to recall some kind of existence *before* the Nothing, it could not.

The little voyager didn't yet know much, but it knew the wind. At least, it knew that this *whoosh* was *called* 'Wind', although they had never been formally introduced. Wind seemed such a formidable Something but, not being able to see it, it was hard to tell what *kind* of a Something it was, and yet it *was* Something.

"Wind?" asked the raindrop, excitedly.

"Talking to me?" blew the wind.

"Um. Where are we going?"

"Oh, hither and thither."

"Whither and what?"

"Ho, ho! Here and there, little raindrop," smiled the gusty one.

Sure enough, the wind seemed to go in one direction for a while and then hold its breath, only to change to another direction for a time before choosing yet *another* direction! The little raindrop couldn't understand why Wind should be so indecisive and thought perhaps it couldn't hurt to ask.

"One has to have variety," said the wind, as though it had read the little one's mind. "Else one becomes bored."

"Oh," thought the little raindrop, feeling that it might possibly have a better chance of *understanding* if it knew what this 'bored' thing was. "What's bored?"

"Bored is a state of 'no change'," stated the wind, importantly.

The raindrop considered this for the longest while but, getting nowhere, it eventually asked politely, "So how does 'no change' become 'bored'?"

"No change + no challenge + no excitement = boredom," blew the clever but invisible Something.

"Well," considered the raindrop aloud, "I've had plenty of change, from the Nothing of before to this whatever I have now... and challenge – I've no idea what that is, but I'm looking forward to whatever's coming next... and I'm excited by this state of suddenly *being*, and then *experiencing* being."

Having summed up its feelings so well, it then realised that 'excited' and 'bored' couldn't possibly share the same space, and so it thought itself not at *all* bored. "Hmm," muttered the raindrop almost to itself, "I understand. Thank you, Wind!"

"You're welcome," breezed the wind.

The wind continued to do what it did best (and it *did* do it rather well, at that) and the little raindrop turned its attention to other things, for there were such things to see! It looked all around itself and saw that everywhere there were others, just like itself, and it could hear the many whoops of joy in all directions; its fellow drops were obviously as happy and excited by this new state of *being* as it was.

Moving its focus away from the others for a while and looking down, the little observer was overwhelmed by the sight spread out below. "Wow!" it exclaimed, pleased that 'wow' seemed rather fitting, as it didn't yet know many other words to explain the feeling it got when words seemed inadequate.

"Wow!" the little raindrop cried again as it looked down at so many different and exciting things. Each thing it saw was so very small that it wasn't obvious what they were supposed to be yet, although there seemed to be a lot of different shades of what it knew to be 'green' down there. Fleetingly it thought, "how do I know green?" but decided that the answer would probably be something similar to how it had known the wind... it just *knew* and the *how* of it didn't seem too important.

The little raindrop shifted its attention away from what it was seeing to how it was feeling as it moved without effort through the soft and gentle air in this amazing place. It felt so happy! Everywhere around it, the wind was playing lazily with the falling raindrops, making them move in all manner of different directions although, whilst playing, it also patiently answered any questions they had – if the answers were within its knowledge, of course.

Looking upward, the little observer noted the underside of the steadily decreasing cloud, hanging in the air above it and, for a fleeting moment, the little one again questioned what had been *before* it had suddenly become aware. With no answer, its attention returned happily to the journey. "Is there anything more beauteous?" it thought in a state

fit to burst with the love of freedom, and of *being*. After a while, however, it didn't seem enough simply to observe and accept without questioning; it wanted to learn. "Wind?" requested the raindrop, calling on the gusty one once more.

"You, again?"

"Yes, it's me. Do you *always* stay here?"

"Here? Good gracious, no – places to go, things to do! But, although I move around, I can be in many parts of the world *at the same time*. Sometimes I'm *not* here; sometimes I'm not elsewhere, but I'm always everywhere."

"You're kidding!"

"It's true. You're seeing, or should I say experiencing, a *part* of what I am now, but I am not just *one* part of me, I am *ALL* of me, and all of me can be all around the world, at once."

"Oh," said the raindrop carefully, obviously not understanding how the wind could do this amazing thing. But, first things first. "What's world?" it asked.

"See down there?"

The raindrop looked at the view below. "Yes."

"Well, that goes on much further than you can see, and all of it together is called the world."

"And you can be in *all* of it, *everywhere?*"

"At once."

"Phew. You know I'm going to have to think about that, don't you?"

"I know."

The little raindrop closed its attention to everything except imagining itself everywhere at once. It tried and tried. And tried. And failed, until it finally admitted, "I can't do it."

"Of course not," said the wind. "You're not Wind, but one day, little raindrop, you will understand that *water* can be everywhere, too. Not today – you're too young – but one day."

"Oh," muttered the little water drop, trying to look less confused than it really was although, strangely, a part of it knew that the wind was right, but didn't know how it *could* be right! "Only a few moments into my existence," it thought, "and I'm baffled already!" Perhaps it was easier just to look at the view.

Down below, more shapes were becoming obvious now and somehow the raindrop knew what they were although, again, it didn't know *how* it knew. Over to the left there was a forest with beautiful, tall, strong trees, reaching upwards to the sky. A silvery river snaked over in the distance, weaving its way through the land and, over to the right, there were yet more trees standing to attention, their leafy arms raised to the sky in a salute to the gentle rain. Everywhere else there seemed to be green squares and oblongs in abundance.

The little raindrop had managed to lose itself in contemplation for quite some time, admiring its surroundings and feeling very happy with its situation, when it suddenly realised, with growing apprehension, that it was floating nearer and nearer to the ground. "Hmm," it thought as it surveyed the changing vista, which was now getting much larger! And very quickly! Things were *so* much closer now.

"Ooooh!" cried the little skydiver, becoming afraid because the ground below was literally *rushing up to meet it*, looming larger and larger with every passing moment. "Oh!" it cried again, as it swished past the tops of the trees and found itself moving to the wind's choreography in a graceful dance, somehow avoiding all the leaves, as it continued on to the earth below.

The landing was a *big* surprise. The tiny traveller hadn't yet experienced **stop**, only **moving**, and it fell heavily into a small puddle, with a loud "ooomph." It was about to concern itself with this when it found it had a lot *more* to worry about, crying out in its mind, "What's *happening* to me? What's happened to my *shape?*"

The raindrop had flattened out, almost to the limits of its being, with its edges bouncing up to form a crown around it. "*Look* at me; I'm *beautiful*," it cried within, torn between feeling really frightened for itself and being amazed by the beauty it saw. This startling new development only lasted a fraction of a second, however, before it found itself moving back to a more recognisable form.

Wondering what this **stop** thing would do next, the little one looked around at all the **moving** raindrops and just about had time to wish it was still one of them before...

"What's this?"

It seemed it was being sucked closer to the surface of the ground and it couldn't understand why it was unable to resist. The little one tried very hard not to have the next stage of its life happen, but happen it did and, in the inevitability of it all, the earth slowly consumed the little raindrop and its fellow travellers.

Very busy still experiencing surprise, the little one shivered. "Oh, I don't think I *like* this," it thought as it quickly slid beneath the surface and was lost to all light and openness. "Yes, I was quite right," it confirmed, "I don't like this at *all!* Where's the light gone? Where's the world? Where's Wind?" it asked silently. Very afraid but trying not to show it, the reluctant explorer drew on all of its reserves of what we would call 'courage' as it felt itself being almost pulled along through this strange, dark place, further and further away from all that it had known.

On and on the little raindrop travelled in the darkness, for what seemed like an endless time, as it struggled to bring its fear under control. "What *is* this place?" it mused. "So unlike the world I knew before. Is this the end result of my beautiful Fall? Am I to stay Here *forever*? Is there to be no more than this? Is this **all**?"

The little voyager wondered and worried as the journey through the dark earth continued and, as time moved on, any hope of being, once again, in its former expansive state slowly faded. This loss of hope left a sadder (almost unhappy) little visitor in this strange, cold place.

ime passed and slowly the little raindrop began to forget the light outside of its current residence, although this concerned it because somehow it thought the light important. "What to do, what to do?" it worried. "What to do?" But there was nothing it *could* do other than to allow the current situation to play through its consciousness. "Ha!" it shouted as it reached a decision (which it felt very smug about). "If I haven't *got* the light, if I can't at this moment *see* the light, then I must try to *imagine* it because *that* would be almost as good… wouldn't it?" With that thought, the clever raindrop paid attention to remembering how it was to be There instead of Here as it concentrated on 'seeing' its beloved light. It concentrated hard.

Nothing happened for the longest while and then, just for a moment, it thought that perhaps…? No. Well, perhaps a little…? No, probably not. **Yes!** There it was! **Light!**

"Where's it coming from?" demanded the raindrop of no one in particular. It didn't quite dare to hope that *it* had accomplished such a difficult task all on its own, but it seemed that it *had* accomplished it. It fell into a grateful silence, a silence with light in it. "Oh, not the kind of light you can *see* by, but the kind you just '*know*' is there," it thought. And, for the first time since encountering this place, the raindrop was happy.

Slowly, the little raindrop began to get used to the slipping, sliding feeling, as it continued its passage through the darkness of its current lodgings, the place it had come to think of as the Here. Certainly, the journey was not without interest. An encounter with a worm had been brief, but enjoyable, and there had been tree roots earlier, but not now. At one point, a giant rock had stood in its way and the little voyager had politely asked the obstruction if it might consider moving.

"Hasn't happened in a long time. Can't see it happening any time soon," the rock had replied. "Sorry."

It had taken the little raindrop quite a while to move around the solid one, bowing to the rock's stature and longevity. But then it was back on its travels, beginning almost to enjoy this odd state of difference that was, by now, far from new.

There was just one thing that saddened it, however, as it travelled on, and it was this: other than the worms, *nothing* Here, in this dark place, had ever *seen* the light, or seen trees (only the roots of them). They had never seen a forest from the air. They had never seen the light shining through a million raindrops, or seen the way Wind moved things. And that was sad, it thought, very sad that deep down within the earth, this place knew nothing of what life was like up There.

In fact, whatever was known Here seemed to be *all* that was known, and that limited truth was then believed to be *All there was* – the Sum Total of Being. Anywhere. No other places, no other worlds in existence but this one. And yet it was obvious, as the little raindrop knew, that the belief had been built up around a falsehood, because this *wasn't* all there was, there was More.

"And they should know that, shouldn't they?" thought the little evangelist, reasonably. "Everything that 'lives' Here ought to be given the chance to know about There." To that end, the little raindrop began to tell everything it encountered (earth, roots, stones, etc.) that there was another state of being, outside of this darkness – a varied, wonderful, *different* sort of life, a life that burst with colour and light everywhere you looked. The worms felt they understood because they had touched upon these truths, but their needs lay basically in the ground and so they had never fully explored the world above.

"Don't you think it's important that *everyone* should know the truth?" asked the little raindrop.

"But *this is* their truth," replied a very patient worm. "We *tried* to tell Here of the other existence, but we were met with such suspicion, doubt and derision that we gave up. Oh, occasionally there are those who *think* there may be Something outside of Here and they question us but, having shared with them the things we've experienced, we are still met with scepticism and mistrust. And those," said the worm incredulously, "are the ones who *want* to know, so what chance do we stand?"

The worms had discovered, in the considerations of the local inhabitants, the solid wall upon which was written:

If I can't see it, I won't believe it.

A solid wall that kept out any light which might otherwise have been discovered. And so it was that a sadder raindrop went about its business, the business of travelling on through the Here and quietly hoping for personal liberation.

It held on to the memory of the light, however, and slowly a new thought filtered through to it, a thought that had a lot to do with choices. It went something like:

> "How I choose to think about my surroundings is going to alter how I react to them. If I decide to think that being Here is a *disaster*, then I shall definitely see it as such. In all probability, with that thought, I shall be become very unhappy."

It then considered the obvious alternative:

> "If I think of this as an *adventure*, I suspect I shall start looking forward to the next thing I may encounter, and the next, and sure enough it will *become* an adventure."

The little thinker was very pleased with the definition of its choices and, having made them clear, it chose one immediately. It decided that its current situation was **not** going to be a *disaster:* it was going to be an *adventure!* Amazingly, from the very moment it decided upon this new idea, its life became *so* much more enjoyable.

Each new day that passed brought the little raindrop something new to discover and often something to learn from. So far, it had met up with a wide variety of the Here dwellers, and had passed some interesting moments talking with them, but its present conversation stood out from all the others – a conversation with a stone, deep within the earth and its darkness.

After the little raindrop had tried at length to explain about There, the stone had fallen into deep thought. "**If**... you are to be believed, and I do mean IF," it said, slowly, "then it would mean that I would have to exhibit Blind Faith, and *choose* to believe what I am being told. With no proof, however, that is entirely too difficult to manage."

"I *know* I'm telling the truth because I've *seen* it!" the frustrated teacher explained, but that, of course, only served to underline the stone's statement.

"That's just what I'm *saying*," the stone said excitedly. "It's *easy* to believe something if you've actually *seen* it, but what if you haven't? How does that work?" The stone paused, awaiting an answer.

"I don't know," the little raindrop whispered, finally. It wished it could find an answer, as it wanted the stone to know the truth, as it did.

"I'm going to have to go away and think about this, but I promise I'll return if I come up with anything of value."

"Fair enough," the stone replied, not really expecting to see the little raindrop again.

The problem was clear: how could someone believe someone else's truth (a truth that *really was* true) if they couldn't see it for themselves? The little raindrop thought and thought, and had very nearly given up thinking about it when the word **trust** began to appear, somewhere in the mists of ignorance. It considered that Trust would have to go something like:

> "I can't see what you can see. I can't see what you *tell* me is there. But I will decide to trust you and *choose* to believe it."

It put this thought to the stone.

"Why, oh why, would I choose to do that?" the stone argued. "And what would be the point of trusting in Something if I never got to see it or interact with it anyway – a Something that will *never* introduce itself to *my* world? To continue living in this darkness, seeing with my own 'eyes' that this is *All There Is*, and yet to believe that out there somewhere is a world of light – well, I ask you, what use is that to me?" the stone asked, in a bewildered sort of way.

"But, if you truly believed there *was* light, you could work to bring a little of it into your daily existence, into the Here," stated the raindrop, with certainty.

"How so, little truth-bringer?" questioned the stone.

"With your *imagination*," said the raindrop knowingly, proceeding to tell the stone how it had brought the light into the Here by imagining it.

"Ha! My point exactly, little raindrop: you must have already **seen** it in order to **recall** it! So it still requires the *Seeing is Believing* principle, doesn't it!" it stated loudly. The stone was triumphant.

"Oh dear," thought the little raindrop, "the stone is not ready, not willing, or not able to take this Leap of Faith. Maybe it couldn't. Maybe it had a point." The little raindrop decided to relax into allowing these Here-dwellers their truth, even if it differed from its own.

With this decision, the raindrop understood the principle called, *Live and Let Live.* It thought, "I don't want anyone telling *me* what to believe; I want to make my *own* mind up. So, if I don't want them doing that to me, what right do *I* have to do that to someone else?" This seemed to equal 'have your truth and allow others to have their own.'

So, even though it knew completely that there *was* More, perhaps it was best not to confuse these Here-dwellers any further by trying to give them something they simply couldn't accept now, or perhaps ever!

The raindrop let go of trying to teach the stone and it moved on, thinking, "I can only explain my truth; I can't make it happen for someone else. The irony is that I've *tried* to explain about the forests to this underground world and they won't believe it, and yet the forest could not exist up There *without* this place! They are so totally interlinked and yet they know nothing of each other's world."

A point had been reached, some time ago, when the raindrop had decided not to fight what *was* anymore, and had slowly begun to resign itself to its current circumstances. Perhaps this was not such a bad place to be; just different. In its own way, Here was just as good as There, and *both* were a part of the All (although it hadn't got a clue what the All was) and somehow, in this thought, the little raindrop found a measure of happiness and contentment.

Recently, nothing much had occurred in this dark place, certainly nothing remarkable or amazing, and nothing that could even be remotely classed as an *adventure*. So it was true to say that, at this moment, the little raindrop was rather bored, thinking of nothing in particular (although, perhaps, the memory of the light was never far from its mind). There was a lot the little traveller didn't know, but perhaps the most important thing it didn't know was that something **big** was about to **happen**. It didn't know this because there was simply no warning.

Suddenly the little raindrop burst free from the confines of the earth and found itself tumbling, rapidly, over rocks, large and small, in the sunshine. "*Wow,*" exclaimed the startled, liberated little being. "Wow, I'm free!" The noise of all the other drops around it blended with its own squeals and whoops of sheer delight.

Such happiness belonged to the little raindrop in that first moment of freedom, and such pleasure at being back in the beloved light! It had never known despair, in the underground world, but it had considered, often, that perhaps it would never see its joyous light again – yet *here it was!* And not only that... it had gained something quite wonderful, for it

now knew the joy of dancing and jostling over these rocks, in the light, as its journey continued. Where was it going? It didn't know. Why was any of this happening? It didn't know *that* either but, right now, in the glory of the day, neither question seemed to beg an answer.

"Wind? It's me again!" called the little raindrop to its earliest friend, "I got lost!"

"I see you," answered the wind, "but, you know, you've *never* been lost, little..."

"Oh yes, I was. I went..."

"Hear me, little one. You were never lost because you were always *with* yourself, so you always knew where you were, didn't you?"

"Yes, but..."

"It's just that you didn't always know where 'where you were' was."

That stopped the little raindrop in its mental tracks. "I'm going to have to think again, you know! You *always* do this to me."

"I know," smiled the wind, who left the little thinker to think. And it didn't take long for the little raindrop to see the wind's point of view, realising happily that his friend, Wind, was right.

"Clever Wind."

The day had been long and wonderful and the tiny traveller's gratitude was great. However, something had been bothering the little raindrop for a while now, something it didn't understand. In fact, the worried one had tried every possible way to ignore its concerns, but it slowly became afraid as the situation worsened. The light was *going out!*

The raindrop had stopped singing and jiggling about and now just allowed itself to be borne along by the steam, feeling tense and scared, its earlier fears now becoming a definite reality. **The light was dying!** The wind had chosen this part of the day to be somewhere else, just when it was needed most, and so the little raindrop just observed this tragedy. Not only was the light dying but it seemed to be connected somehow to the light-disc in the sky. It had gone from being a bright, golden colour, to a more muted red, and now seemed to be turning a cold, dull, pinkish grey. In fact, it was becoming harder for the little raindrop to see the path of the stream at all.

The worried raindrop looked back up at the light-disc and, just when it thought things couldn't get any worse... it saw the light-disc *being slowly eaten by the trees!* "No, please; let the light live!" cried out the near-distraught little observer.

"Don't worry."

"Who spoke?" asked the little raindrop, looking all around in the fading light.

"Me," replied a very large leaf that had recently fallen onto the water's surface. The raindrop had seen it earlier but was rather preoccupied by the tragedy of the moment.

"Don't worry about the sun," the leaf continued.

"What's 'sun'?" interrupted the student, unhappily watching the light-disc's death throes in the trees.

"The sun is that big round circle of light going down behind those trees."

"*Behind* the trees? You mean it's not being *eaten* by them?"

"Eaten?" the leaf chuckled, "good heavens, no. It's going somewhere else. This happens every night."

"What's 'night'?" asked the little raindrop, almost embarrassed by its obvious ignorance.

"Night is what you call the resultant darkness while the sun is busy being somewhere else," said the leaf knowingly.

"Oh," digested the raindrop. "So what's the light part called then, when the sun's here?"

"Wind says it's called day. But it's not always very light; sometimes the clouds roll in and the light is trapped behind them, not completely, but trapped all the same."

"I came from a cloud," stated the little cloud particle, solemnly.

"I came from a tree," the leaf said with some sadness about not being attached to a tree any longer. "But I'm enjoying this stream and, although I've no idea where I'm going, I'm just enjoying the journey."

"That's what I think, too," the raindrop agreed. With night clouds already rolling in, it couldn't see much of the leaf anymore, just the dark shape of it, which started it thinking about the sun again. "When will the sun return?"

"Tomorrow," promised the dark leaf. "It'll come back tomorrow."

"Good." The little raindrop didn't know what 'tomorrow' was but the leaf had sounded certain that the sun would return, and that was all the little questioner needed to know. The darkness surrounding it now was quite unlike the darkness of the cold earth but the little raindrop settled into it and waited, trusting the leaf implicitly.

any days and many nights went by and, as the time passed, a wonderful feeling of gratitude began to sink into the little raindrop. In its new-found life, it spent many happy days lying on its back, looking at the often-gentle sky. This was the same sky that never tired of the barrage of questions fired silently at it (never *answering* any, but seeming to listen all the same) – the same sky that had somehow given life to the little raindrop.

There were other days spent racing and whooping around over the rocks, with its other little friends, thinking of nothing other than simply having fun. On days like those, the raindrop knew pure joy.

This day, however, was a thinking day, when the little philosopher was thinking, once again, of Here and There, and of how the words changed, depending upon which side of the fence you were standing at the time. The Light Place, which it had thought of as There when under the ground, had now become Here, and the little raindrop wondered if *everyone's* truth was relative to their current situation. It supposed so.

"How happy I am," the little one said aloud, on this 'thinking' day, "and how wonderful all this is. I wonder...?" But its thinking processes were cut short when its circumstances changed yet again, without a fanfare or a whisper of warning. Quite suddenly it had struck a rock at an odd angle and had ricocheted onto another low rock, overhanging the river in which it had previously been travelling. The hapless one landed towards the back of the rock amongst others whom the same fate had befallen, and now sat there, waiting.

"Oh, help," it whispered.

Nothing happened as the little raindrop sat on the rock in silence and waited. And waited. It was going nowhere although, after a while, it wondered if it *may* have been moving forward, almost imperceptibly, but it wasn't sure. The little raindrop was in shock. "What if this is **it**?" it thought, with the same foreboding it had felt about its underground excursion. "What if I am never able to rejoin my fellow droplets in the stream again? What if I have now lost my wonderful freedom, the freedom to play in the soft, bubbling water in the sunlight?" It fell silent.

After an age on the ledge, the stranded raindrop looked within, asking many questions to see if it could learn anything from the knowledge it had gained. Perhaps, eventually, a solution to its current dilemma might be found from within itself. However, before it got around to considering all the things it *knew*, it thought about all the things it *didn't* know – all those questions that needed answers – and among them were:

"What *was* the cloud and where had it come from? Had it *always* been there?"

"Where was I *before* I fell from the cloud, and if I don't remember, does it matter?" The raindrop felt that it *did* matter, but it wasn't sure why. "Oh, and why is it that I don't remember what came before? Could it be that once there was Nothing, and from Nothing came Something?" The raindrop was a picture of concentration as it sat there, stranded, on the ledge.

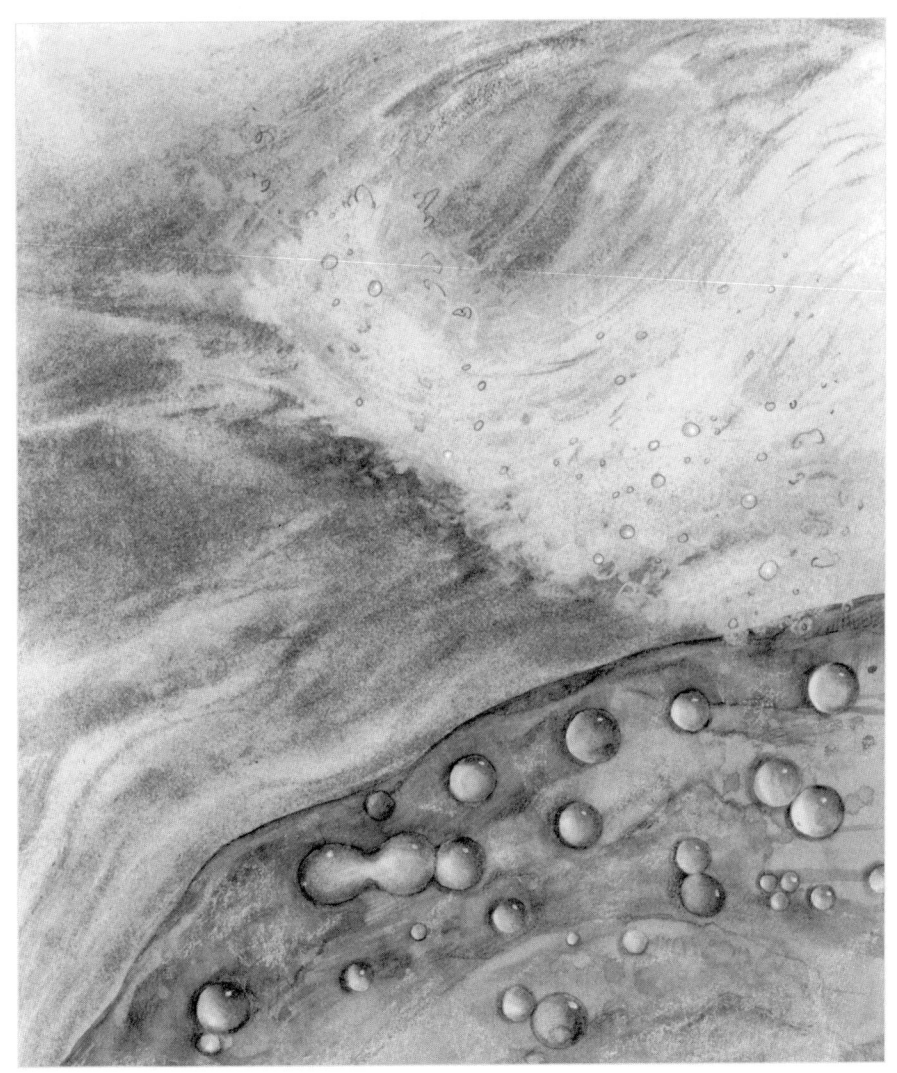

"Still questioning?" asked the wind, gently.

"Hmmm," answered the seeker, "but I'll find my answers, I know I will."

"Oh, I don't doubt it."

These questions (that came without answers) had begun to excite the little raindrop, in a challenging sort of way. It wondered perhaps if this was the time to discuss these things with its fellow droplets, as it seemed no one was going anywhere just at the moment. It also wanted to create a feeling of unity among these other drops and hopefully spark a conversation, as it found this current silence quite unsettling.

It began to ask a few of the other stranded drops on the ledge if they knew the answers. Most of them, it seemed, hadn't even *considered* questioning things (seeming simply to accept what *was* and just get on with it) and no one knew any of the answers, although a few began guessing and some fables were born, confusing everyone. Perhaps it didn't pay to guess about such things and yet, without speculating, how else...?

While the What-Was-the-Nothing-Before-it-Became-the-Something? argument raged, the raindrop gradually closed itself to the debate it had begun and floated mentally out and above the furore. Still in an effort to understand, it tried gently to put everything together. "Now let me see," it thought:

"I know I suddenly became conscious of floating free in the sky, way above the earth. I remember looking around me and seeing what my limited knowledge considered to be the 'whole picture' from on high, and I thought my time there would go on forever.

"The moment I considered that all I could see was *All There Was*, things changed and the ground came rushing up to swallow me, taking away my lovely light and freedom.

"When I started to think that my home would be permanently in the cold, dark earth, things changed again, and I burst free of my confines, out into the stream. Splashing around with my fellow droplets, I thought that *that* would last forever, too.

"Now everything's changed, yet again, and I find myself stranded on a ledge, wondering if *this* situation will last forever?

"So, from all these things I know, what have I learned?" The little raindrop checked its findings, and its findings were thus:

"I don't know what came before, but I Am, **now**, and my Now is ever changing. So, it's not wise to consider my life stagnant because nothing has so far stayed the same, but that doesn't seem to be a bad thing. OK. So if my **now**s change and always seem to become something else, then I won't be stuck on this ledge forever, will I?" The little philosopher suddenly brightened and began to relax and soon found itself almost enjoying lying on the rocky ledge. It no longer saw itself as being 'stranded', more that it was simply *having another adventure*, albeit one that didn't take it very far!

The debate it had begun, between itself and the other drops, had run out of steam, and the only conversation to be overheard now was the occasional welcoming and calming of the newcomers by the established ledge-dwellers. The little raindrop listened for a while but it was missing the sound of the stream, from *inside* the stream, and not just on top, like this, where the sound was very different. It had just set about recreating the sound within itself, in the same way as it had recreated the light, when it heard, "Reach out to me, you're close. I'll reach out to you. If we can join forces we may be heavy enough to roll to the edge of the rock and rejoin the stream." It seemed a good idea.

"OK," agreed the raindrop. It applied its mind and imagined itself a fraction away from where it was and a fraction nearer to the other drop.

It imagined hard, and long, and really thought that at one point it *had* moved. It tried and tried but it was no use. Neither of them had managed to get any closer to the other and, just when they were both about to give up, a new raindrop ricocheted out of the stream and fell onto the rock, landing so close to the little raindrop that they touched, just.

"Oh, help," said the new drop.

"I said that!" exclaimed the little welcoming committee. "But don't worry; we have a plan to move together, back into the stream."

"Uh, OK. What do I have to do?" asked the new recruit to the plan.

"Well it seems that you might have already done it!" exclaimed the little raindrop. It found itself drawn more and more towards the new drop and the one beside it until, quite suddenly, they all joined forces and moved together very quickly. A small pebble parted their togetherness for a moment, but it didn't hinder their forward momentum, which was just enough to allow them to plunge back into the stream, soon joyously singing and jumping as before.

But things were *not* as before; now there were *more* questions, which no one could answer. And they needed answers. The raindrop now wanted to know if there was a purpose, or a reason, or a sense behind all things and, if so, what was it? "I learned to relax into my circumstances and have patience with that last adventure," it considered. "I also now recognise a pattern of changes taking place in my existence, and I have learned that *chance* (with the arrival of the new drop) can make things *happen*. So, is there some Greater Plan at work here? If there is, and I allow myself to go along with life, wherever it may take me, then I may well be *led* to the answers I seek," it said importantly.

With that the little raindrop knew Wisdom.

*A*fter many sunlit days spent playing in the stream, the stream had become a river, and running and whooping over small rocks had become a thing of the past. Often, as the sun set each night, the little one watched as it was being 'eaten by the trees' and laughed at its younger self, remembering the kind leaf who had helped it to understand.

A part of the river now and yet still very much itself, the little raindrop settled into a different lifestyle. This part of its life seemed to involve playing less and simply moving in the main body of water, with the others, in a much more determined sort of way. Why? It didn't know. Where was it going? It didn't know that either, but it relaxed fully into enjoying this new and somewhat amazing feeling of unity with its fellow drops.

Today was a good day, a typically 'lazy' day when the clouds, what few there were, crawled slowly across the sky, and the breeze was gentle. The only thing that seemed to move quickly every now and again was the sun, which appeared to race across the land each time a small cloud moved across it.

On this lazy day, the little raindrop closed its conscious state to everything but simply allowing itself to be borne along by the others in the river, knowing that this latest change was good, for it led somewhere, it was certain. It led to the *next stage*, although the little raindrop had no idea what that might be but, whatever it was, it carried with it a strong sense of wanting to fulfil its purpose. Of course, the next mild concern was that it didn't *fully* understand 'purpose' but it knew the idea. And it knew that somewhere on the end of 'purpose' it would find fulfilment. Soon.

When the little raindrop chose to open its awareness and look around again, some time later, it noted that the clouds had thickened and that they were now displaying hints of grey instead of the beautiful fluffy white they had been before. "Not that shades of grey aren't every bit as beautiful, in their own way," it thought. "After all, didn't *I* come from one just like them?" It smiled at the clouds and then looked lazily around at the banks, reassuring itself that things were just as they should be before it then surveyed the path ahead.

"What are *those?*" the startled one asked in a mixture of interested and fearful surprise. Ahead, there was a fragmented group of very large and oddly shaped Somethings, which wouldn't have bothered the little adventure-drop at all except for the one, small fact that some of them *were in the water!* It hoped fervently that they would be *out* of the water before it got there, because getting there was inevitably what it was very busy doing.

While the concerned traveller still had time to ponder on whether it had a problem or not, it remembered a certain someone who *might* just be able to help. "Wind?" it called out, in the hopes that its first friend might hear.

"Not heard from you for a while."

"No, I suppose I've been answering my own questions, given time..."

"Ah, as it should be," interrupted the wind.

"...but right now there's something I need to know, and I thought you might be able to help me."

"If I can," agreed the gusty one, waiting.

"Those... Somethings... down there. What are they? It's just that I've not seen them before, and I seem to be heading straight towards them."

"Oh, they're called 'cows' by the tall ones."

"Tall ones?"

"The tall ones call themselves 'humans'. I got 'sun' and 'night' from them, too. Humans seem to have many questions, like you, with very few answers but, *unlike* you, they seldom ask Wind or Sun, or the All, about their really big issues... but that's another story." The wind got itself back on track to answer the current question. "When you meet the cows, if you are near enough to them, they might drink you. But that's not a bad thing. In fact it's one of the reasons why you have come into this life."

"What, to get *drinked?*" asked the raindrop, slightly alarmed about its lack of knowledge on the subject. If the cow *did* choose to drink it, then its fate would be sealed, wouldn't it? And if that was to be the case, shouldn't it know *exactly* what that entailed? "Uh, what'll happen to me if I do get drinked?"

"Drunk. You'd get drunk."

"Sorry."

"You'd go inside the cow and give her life; you'd help her to live because that's part of what Water does. In fact," said the wind humbly, bowing to its truth, "Water is so much more important to the All than I am."

The little raindrop couldn't believe the wind's last words and argued, "But you know *so* much more than me; how come I mean more to the All? That can't be right."

"Knowledge and experience are good things, little one, but ultimately it isn't whether you're clever or not that makes you important to the All – it's how you *live* your life, and what you may bring to it, and to others around you."

"A thinking moment is needed," the raindrop joked, hoping to hide its confusion, but it didn't get very far with that. Quite soon it continued, "So this 'giving life' stuff that I can do for the cow – is that the same kind of giving life that the cloud did for me? Because if I believed I were as clever as the cloud, I could get awfully proud and not-nice-to-know, you know!"

The wind looked fondly on this questioning drop of water and it said, gently, "There are many ways to give life, little one: this is one way, the cloud was another. They are no less important than each other. Look upon it as an honour to give the cow life. But I'll tell you something – you won't fully understand the meaning of 'giving life' until you're actually doing it. There's really *nothing* I can say that will prepare you for the feeling."

The little raindrop hesitated, wanting to know and yet afraid to ask, "Have you... I mean, have you ever...?"

"No," answered the wind simply and quietly. "But I feel it somehow, when all of you manage to do it. In some way that I don't really understand, I *do* feel it."

"I'm glad," said the little raindrop, meaning it deeply. The wind fell silent and the raindrop gazed back in the direction of the cows and realised, with an escaping "Oh," that it was a lot nearer to them than it had been.

Although the clouds were gathering quickly, it had been a warm day so far, and the cow had not drunk for some hours. Already standing up to her knees in the water, she lowered her large nose and opened her mouth in anticipation of the delicious coolness she would soon taste. It was surprising, in such a large animal, that she was so delicate and gracious about the way she drank. Gently drawing in large mouthfuls of water, she slaked her thirst, her ears twitching and her tail flicking with the joy of it all.

Meanwhile, unavoidably, borne along by the river, the little raindrop was heading straight into the cow's path. She was just lifting her soft mouth from the delicious coolness when the raindrop inevitably collided with her and ended up clinging, precariously, to her nose.

With one last look around, the cow turned and climbed up the bank, up onto the soft grass to join the others of its kind. "What a strange new quietness," its passenger thought. "A quietness most unlike the silence of the deep earth." All around, new raindrops were floating down from the sky, beginning their own life experiences. The little raindrop looked up from its strange location at the new recruits. It surprised itself as it realised that it felt strangely parental towards them, thinking lovingly, "I wonder what lies ahead for all of you, on your travels, and what you might encounter? And will you *have* travels, or will most of you simply slide into the cool earth and be lost from the light forever?"

Suddenly sliding down the host's nose, the startled raindrop once again floated through the air for a short time, until it landed on the top of a wide blade of grass.

"We're off!" it thought gleefully, preparing itself for yet more adventures, but time passed and the little raindrop, try as it might, remained where it was. It couldn't shift. "OK," it thought, as it tried not to worry about its new situation and held on to what it had learned: "Nothing stays the same forever. All things change, eventually." Although,

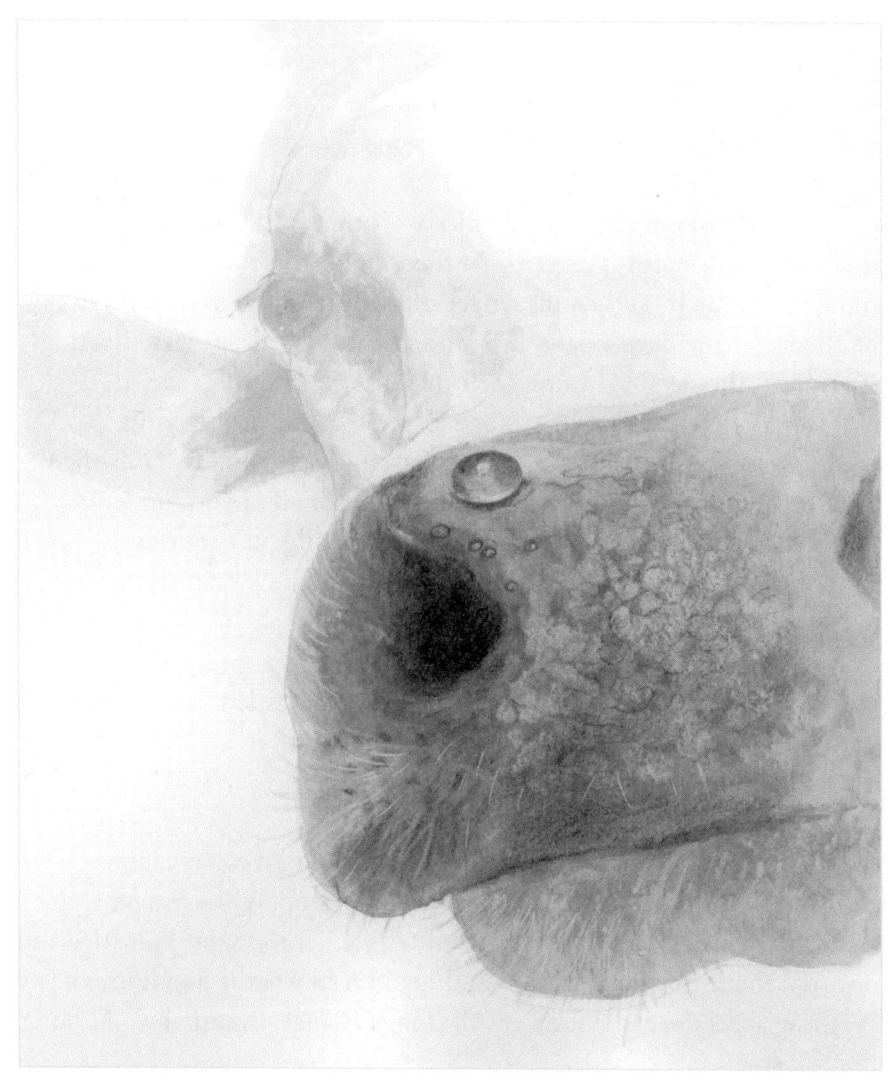

48

cheekily, it urged of fate, "Soon, please! Let me move soon, and then I can be on my way again."

Time passed and nothing happened as the raindrop waited, gaining precious little in the way of patience. "This is going to be an *adventure*," it reminded itself, and promptly decided to overcome its enthusiasm for the 'next step' by applying itself to exploring where it was right now. "It seems pleasant enough here," it thought, looking around at its immediate surroundings from this vastly different perspective. The blade of grass was obliging and the rain was easing, and a watery sun smiled down on the land. "It's really quite nice."

Slowly, the peace and quiet of its new location got through to the raindrop, and its need to be moving on abated, just a little. It had the strange feeling that everything else around it was just content to be here, nothing wanting to *be* anywhere else or *do* anything else. All the many aspects of life appeared to be just getting on with their various co-dependent societies.

To the stranded one, the wondrous freedom of the river was now becoming both a memory and a hope for the future...

The rain was easing considerably now and the little voyeur sat on the blade of grass in the strengthening sun. It became aware as it sat there that strange things were happening, things that were both incredible and yet disconcerting. As it looked into itself, it became aware of a range of the most exquisite colours: red, orange, yellow, green, blue, indigo, violet... ."*How amazing!*" it cried. And yet, this change did *not* alter the raindrop that it was. As it lifted its gaze upward, it saw the same wondrous colours, in a giant arc across the sky and, for a while, the little raindrop forgot its current restrictions and became quite lost in its joy.

"What is in me is in the Greater Sky," thought the raindrop, looking from the arc, to itself, and back again. "The lesser is reflected in the Greater, the Greater in the lesser." It felt that this realisation had brought it nearer to *some* kind of understanding about its existence, but it wasn't sure how. A deep satisfaction and a feeling of awe spread through the raindrop, and it fell into a peaceful reverie... which lasted until the bird landed.

The blackbird had a nest filled with fledglings and those eager little ones needed food, lots of food. With sharp eyes, the bird watched the ground, pushing repeatedly into the wet earth and pulling out its prize of worms. With two wriggling worms already lined up and hanging over the sides of the merciless beak, it thrust into the ground again, very near the raindrop and, as it retreated, it was clear that it had won yet another prize.

The worms wriggled and twisted, struggling hard against their fate and, in doing so, one hapless worm transferred the little raindrop onto its ridged back. What happened next was over in a moment: the bird opened its wings and flew, soaring into the sky, as the worm carrying the little raindrop gave another magnificent wriggle and the raindrop was ejected from some height. And the direction was down, once again, moving freely through the unresisting air.

Without too much time to think, the much-travelled raindrop found itself the uninvited guest, this time, of a flower, at least for a few moments, as it landed on it and then slid down the stem to the base where, once again, it knew the darkness of the earth. Its progress, however, into the deeper soil was halted by a very delicate root, drawing the drop gently along inside of itself, so gently in fact that it felt invited.

During its stately progression into the flower, the little visitor had time to reflect. It thought that of all of the numerous events that had brought it to this moment, *none* of them had given it the feeling that was beginning to dawn within it now – a feeling of purpose and destiny. "Was this what the wind meant?" it asked silently.

It noticed that the root was becoming wider as it was drawn on and on, until there was a sense of a dull green glow in the darkness. The glow was above it at first but then gradually spread all around it, and the raindrop knew it was within the same stem it had slid down some time before. Somehow, slowly, its consciousness was beginning to change! It realised it could *feel* the plant – not just the stem but the leaves, the buds, the flowers, the roots – and the feeling was... serene.

This was different from anything it had experienced to date: it was different from flying through the air; being in the earth in the darkness; flowing in the stream; being in the sun; being in the river. All those things, it decided, were still a raindrop *being a raindrop*. Not at all like Now.

The little raindrop realised that its life force was slowly merging with

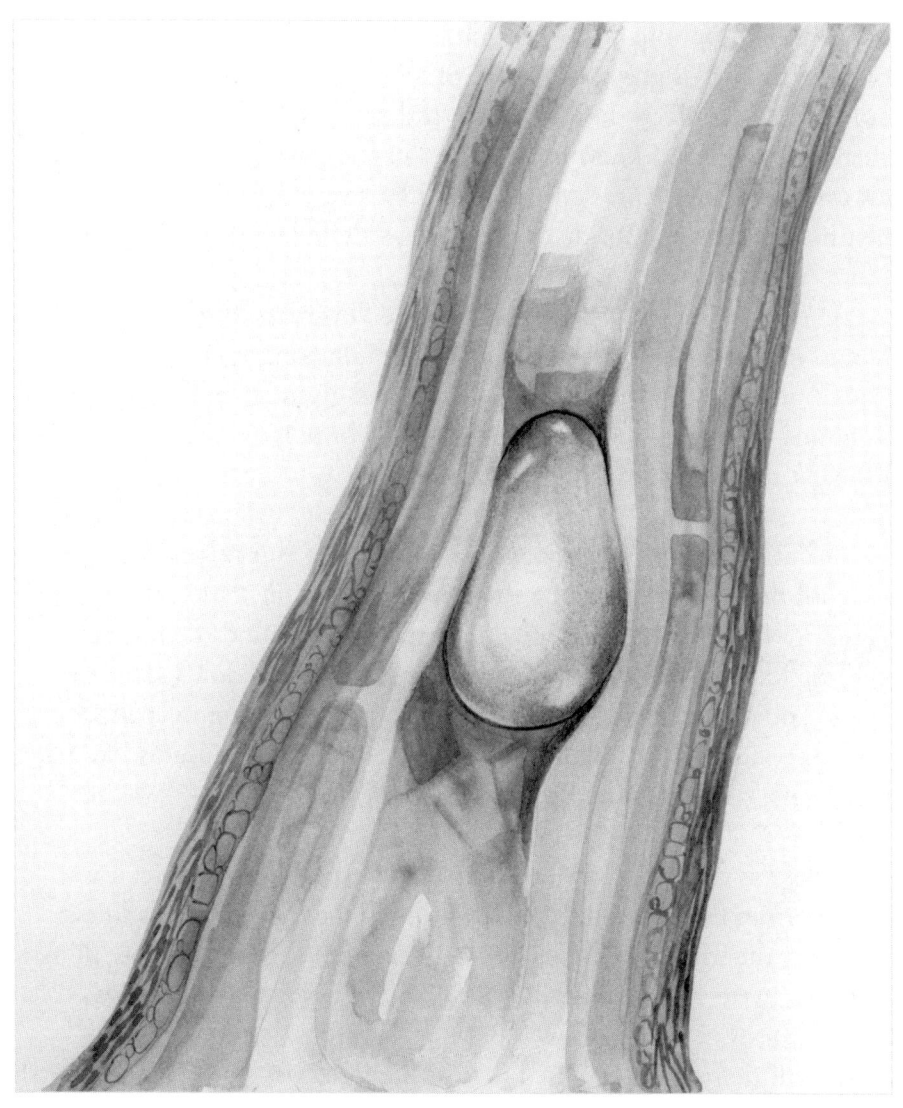

the life force of this gentle being; it felt as though it was allowing the plant to live, by laying down its individuality and joining its forces with Nature herself. The raindrop thought it had known joy in the river, or with the Rainbow, but now...? Well, it thought it might just have to burst with the joy it felt at this moment! "Yes, Wind, yes," it shouted, "*This is important!* You were so right."

Slowly, so slowly, the little raindrop was experiencing being the flower in its totality, even seeming to share the flower's memory of its seeding and its growth. It felt what the flower felt, and what it felt was *amazing*: the gentle breeze playing over the millions of tiny 'hairs' on its stem, and leaves. Sounds filtered through in a muffled but somehow very obvious way, sounds of life – birdsong in abundance as well as the sounds of the nearby river. The little raindrop had never experienced anything like it and, as the warmth of the sun soaked in all around, its joy was deep and its gratitude boundless.

In this state of peace it thought, "So far in my life I have known *many* states of existence, and now this. What more *is* there for me to experience? Will I go on changing, I wonder, or have I arrived at this place, this time, to stay here forever to help this flower to live? Is my journey over? Have I arrived? Oh, and what is *forever?*"

Its questions went unanswered, for the moment.

The little raindrop was aware that, although it was now also undeniably a part of the flower, it still had separate consciousness, and it was still being drawn upward, through the beautiful dim green light. "How wonderful," it thought. "To sit in a field by a river, being a flower and yet still a raindrop."

Slowly, the little voyager was sucked, gently, into a narrow tube; this it knew to be the part of the flower that attached the leaf to the main stem. Its journey through the tube was not long before... more change. The raindrop was gently stretched and lengthened and separated into three, four, five thin veins at once. It was warmer here, and there was a strange sensation, an odd vibration that filled it with mirth: the ant was making its way along the underside of the leaf, unaware of the effect it was having!

Within the leaf, the raindrop lay separated and yet at one (both with the other parts of itself *and* with the flower). "Now, how can this be," it thought, "that I am water and this flower is *separate* from what I am, and yet we can be as one?" Bonded as it was with this flower, the seeker of life's answers was coming nearer, with every passing moment, to feeling that it had found the reason for its existence.

"Wind? I'm *giving life*," cried the little one with profound gratitude, but there was no acknowledgement from its absent friend. "You *are feeling* this with me, aren't you?" it hoped. "You said you could."

The little raindrop concentrated on a strange and different feeling that was surfacing within it. "I feel..." It struggled to find the right words. "Oh, how *do* I feel?" it asked, sighing. "But what am I doing? I have to

allow the *feeling* to find *me*, instead of searching so hard to find *it*." And, with a little time spent simply being with the feeling, a single descriptive word finally emerged. "That's it," the raindrop said reverently. "I feel fulfilled."

As it settled into the depth of this new discovery, the raindrop knew that, through this lovely flower, it had found its destiny and, on this day of its life, it had come to know complete peace.

The bark came from a distance, but it moved closer and closer. An excited bark, an excited dog, for he could *see* and *smell* the water now, and his owner was experiencing difficulty in keeping up the chase. The dog passed by some way to the left of the little flower... and the owner? The owner's boot came swiftly through the air, on a collision course with the leaf that housed the little raindrop. The curled leaf had been *so* close to the ground that it made it easy for the boot to crash down on the edge of it, causing both the leaf and the stem to be nearly squashed, with the leaf breaking almost in half. It was only the softness of the earth beneath the leaf that saved it from being crushed altogether. The boot and its owner went on their way, unaware of this tiny tragedy, and the owner of the bark moved excitedly into the near distance, still quite obviously demented at his prospects!

All the parts of the raindrop began oozing slowly out of the broken leaf and started to collect along the edge. At the time of the damage, the raindrop had felt the shock go right through the plant and itself but, although the leaf was broken, the raindrop knew at once that the plant would survive, and it felt calmed by this knowledge.

It was strange but already the little raindrop felt that its special connection with the plant was waning; no longer did it feel *at one* with it and part of it. The broken part of the leaf was *here* whereas the life force of the plant now seemed to be *over there*; they were no longer connected. "I didn't expect that," thought the little raindrop, and went on to think that, perhaps, only when it merged its will with the Greater Need was it to feel part of something other than itself. The Greater Need, in this case, had been to keep the plant alive.

At length, the little raindrop fully emerged from the damaged leaf and, due to the leaf's angle, it began sliding down towards the earth, joining up again as one single drop before it landed on the mossy grass. After a while of wondering what was to be next, and feeling lonely in its singular state, it attempted to feel part of the grass, as it had felt part of the flower, but it was no use. "I'm not *within* it, *at one* with it," thought the little Buddhist. "I'm not part of its life force: I'm outside of it." It desperately wanted to feel part of something again, to belong.

As though it had heard the desperate need, the sun came out from behind a cloud at just that moment, and it beat down upon the little lost one, loving it and warming it thoroughly until, quite outside of its own doing, the little one stopped worrying and started to relax.

A deep and wonderful feeling was stirring within the little raindrop. It began to feel different somehow, but was unable to understand the change. It closed its mind to all but the sunshine and enjoyed the experience, finding itself no longer yearning for the flower, in fact no longer worrying about anything. "Such a wonderful feeling," it thought. A wonderful feeling that went on blissfully for some time until it realised that *something was happening!*

Suddenly startled, the raindrop felt itself both where it was, on the ground, but also *around* itself, in the air, *at the same time*. How could

this be? Opening its consciousness to its watery state, it scanned itself and was horrified to discover that it was now much smaller than it had been, and yet it felt *more* of whatever it was that it had been, feeling that it was growing and expanding. "But, how...?"

The sun beat down, and the raindrop was both afraid for its decreasing self and yet very happy. It didn't know how it could be both at once. If it focused on itself as water, it became afraid because it was dying. If it focused on itself as a kind of expansive Something, that was *not* physical, well then its pleasure knew no bounds.

"What *is* this? What's happening to me?" cried what was left of the little raindrop, and what was left was not very much at all. Yet the raindrop felt it was somehow *everywhere* in the air above the grass, hovering over where the very last of it remained in the hot sunlight. It now appeared to be *hundreds* of tiny droplets, all resembling the drop that it had once been. No, not hundreds: thousands – perhaps millions. Each droplet, of itself, appeared to be experiencing something slightly different from the rest, and yet it could still access the conscious state that it knew as The Little Raindrop.

The greater parts looked down at the last part and said, "Come."

The last part said, "I am afraid of dying, of letting go of what I have experienced here, of what it means to **be** here."

The Higher Self said gently, "Come home, little one," with more love than the little raindrop thought it could ever know.

It let go.

"What am I?" it thought. "Somehow 'I' have changed. I used to be 'me'. But what *was* 'me'?" Parts of itself were everywhere. It could clearly see the whole of the river by now, with endless varieties of beautiful flowers, each one adding their own gift of colour to the land. It paused, taking a moment to recall the gentleness of the flower that had shown it the meaning of its life – all the parts of it clearly and fondly remembering. But, for all *that* experience had been amazing, it couldn't beat what the endless parts of itself were feeling right now.

With a final smile at the flowers, it continued its visual explorations. It could see the forests it had glimpsed on its original Fall from the cloud. It could see the fields beyond; oh and cows, many cows, sprinkled in those fields. It could see concrete, soulless shapes beyond that, and beyond those it could see yet more fields and trees. At any time it found that it was able to switch its attention to other areas, without losing whatever else it had concentrated on. Somehow it could do it all at once. "*Wow!* I had been so afraid of letting go," and now it wondered why.

The cosmic raindrop turned its attention to the sun. "Where am I going?" it asked politely.

"You are going back to help form a new cloud," said the sun.

"You mean... *I* helped to form the *old* one?" asked the student of life, humbly.

"Yes."

"Oh. *Oh!*"

"Sun?" asked the raindrop, after a suitable time of being completely confused.

"Yes?"

"What has just happened to me? You know: the Fall; the land; the river. All that. What was that?"

"An existence; a life, if you will."

"But *why?*" shouted the needy one.

"Why, what?" asked the sun, patiently.

"Why did I need to *do* all that? What was it all for? Why couldn't I just have stayed part of the cloud, and looked down on it all?"

"Would you have learned, little one?"

"Learned?"

"Could you have learned all that you know now, if you'd stayed in the cloud, do you think?"

Silence. All the millions of parts of what the raindrop had now become thought about this.

"There is ignorance," said the sun, after a suitable time, "and there is knowledge. To learn, you have to *experience*. To experience, you have to *do*. In doing, you may *learn*. In learning, you may *grow*."

"What, into a bigger cloud?" asked the student.

"No, little one, you can grow into a greater understanding of who and what you are, and your place in the All."

"What's the All?"

"Everything."

"Huh?"

"You are *part* of the All. Your experiences, your knowledge is 'transmitted' to the All, and the All continues to expand, to understand, and to grow with all the information It receives."

"You mean, I am more than just a part of a cloud, and sustenance for a flower?" asked the little raindrop, quietly.

"What do you think?" the sun asked, waiting to see what its student had learned.

"I think I must be important... and yet... not important at all."

"How so?" asked the sun.

"Well, whatever I learn should be of *some* importance to this All, and yet I am not important as myself, as a raindrop, I am only important because of what I can bring, in the way of learning, to the rest?" This last sentence was asked as a kind of question, and yet the little raindrop knew that what it had said was true.

"But you *are* important, little one, very important," said the sun, gently. "And yet, you are right. No one component, no one part of something greater than itself can have self-importance, and yet the All cares about each component deeply. It cares for *you*, your needs and your possibilities. It cares who you are, how you are, and whether you have goodness within you or not. It desires your wellness, your happiness, your freedom to learn, or *not* to learn, as you see fit."

"You mean, if you *don't* learn, that's all right too?"

"Only for a while. A very long while, but only for a while," said the sun, mysteriously.

"What happens then?" The little raindrop wasn't sure it wanted an answer to its question.

The sun had fallen silent, and the raindrop had time to reflect. "I suppose if I were asking someone to come and join me, in a place where there was love and goodness, and they didn't want to come, I wouldn't push them," thought the raindrop. "But what would I do if they still didn't want to come, after a very long time? I suppose I would honour their choice, and be there without them."

"That's about it," said the sun.

"You can *hear* me?"

"I have heard all your thoughts throughout your last existence, little one, and before that. I know you. You are of me."

The consciousness of the raindrop/mist looked deep into the sun, and found the rainbow. It looked deeper and it found the cloud. Deeper still, and it found the earth and the sky. "*You* are the All!"

"I Am," said the sun. "And so are you. We are all One."

"Oh." A little word that tried to convey *so* much, spoken so quietly that it was almost silent. "Oh."

The raindrop was feeling strange. Very high in the air now, each part of itself seemed to be surrounded by many other such parts. It seemed that each conscious thought that it had could be understood by these other parts, and (more amazingly) *it* could understand *their* thoughts! Each other part seemed to be a friend, known to the little raindrop, and yet a stranger at the same time – and yet not a stranger at all. The little raindrop tried to be confused, but it was feeling very clear – it wasn't sure of what it thought it knew yet, but it was very clear.

The one thing that it *was* sure of, in amongst all this uncertainty and newness, was that it was changing in a way that couldn't be stopped or fought against. And before 'whatever it was' that was going to happen next happened, there was Someone it needed to talk with.

"Wind?"

"Yes, my friend?"

The little raindrop was very touched because although it had thought of the wind as its friend, it never realised that Wind felt the same in return. "Thank you," said the mist proudly.

"For what?"

"For being my friend."

"Oh, you're easy to like," said the wind. "You're even easier to love."

In that second the sun burst free from a nearby and higher cloud and shone through the mist particles, highlighting them all. The cosmic one was pleased with the Sun's timing as 'shining with light' was what it felt it was doing on the inside too. "It's *all* about love, isn't it?" questioned One who understood.

"Yes, little one, it *is* all about love."

After a pause the raindrop/mist continued, "I wanted to say 'goodbye' because I felt that whatever I *was,* was changing, and I wondered if I would be Here afterwards. Uh, will I?"

"What you have just done," answered the wind, "the life that you have just lived, will never come again because it's already been... it's already become a part of the All. The *really important* things that you have learned have been integrated too and won't need to be learned again. But You will never cease to be, in some form or other..."

"...because if I ceased to be, the All would cease to be, too!"

"Exactly. You used to have to think about things," the wind reminded fondly.

"I know."

There was a pause as the two friends tried to hold back the inevitable and yet welcome it at the same time. "I'll say 'goodbye' then, until we meet again," the wind said softly.

"Before you go, one more thing. Will *you* do this? Will this kind of change happen to *you?*"

The wind replied, "There are many levels of being and they are all quite different from each other."

The wind had not finished what it was saying but in that split second the raindrop/mist knew, without doubt, that the stone beneath the earth had its *own* wonder; its own beauty in its own way, and no less valid than this. "Of *course!*" it thought as it realised why the stone could never believe in the light. It wasn't part of its reality and it didn't *need* to be because the stone's *own* truth was just as beautiful; it had been quite correct in questioning the use of knowing such a different state.

The raindrop then realised that there must be many different types of existence, and that *its* reality, the wind's and the stone's were only three of them. They all had their own truth and each truth was valid and yet differed from the other. "So truth *is* relative," it knew at last.

The wind continued, "We are *all* different from each other. Well, take you and me – I am a *constant* whereas you..."

"...are a visitor!" interrupted the visitor.

"Yes, I suppose so."

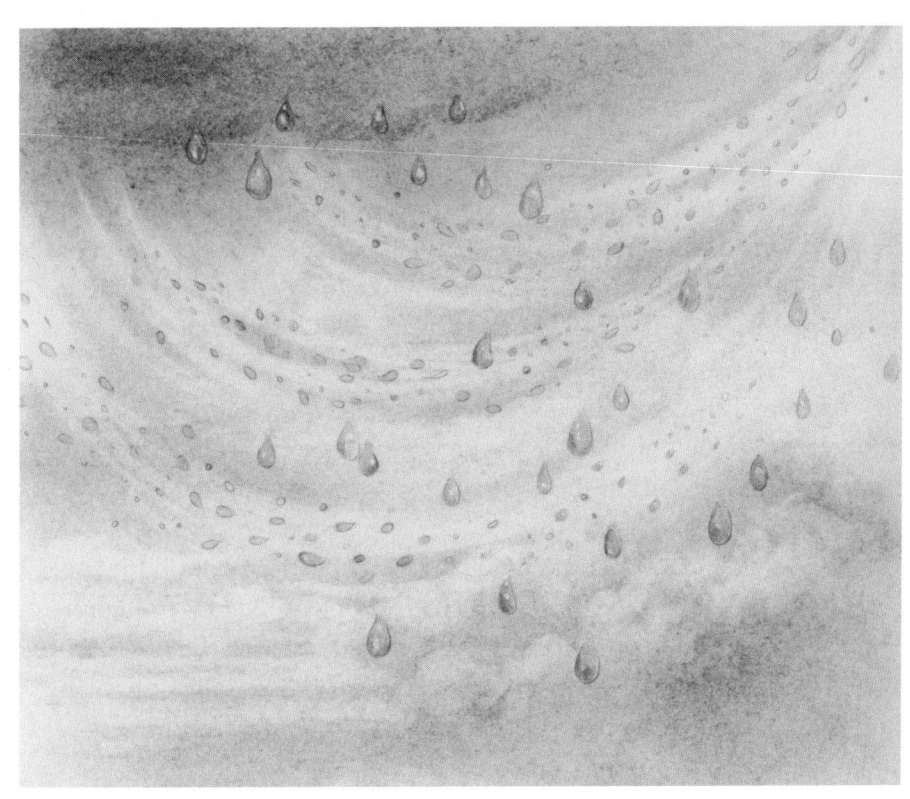

"So you are a constant. The All is a constant, too, so you are nearer to the All than you thought," teased the raindrop/mist, knowingly.

"I *am* the All," replied the wind, "but then, you know that by now, don't you?"

"Oh, yes, the sun told me. *We're* ***all*** *the All, in our different ways.*"

They both fell silent as they knew that the moment had come for the wind to be somewhere else but, before it departed it blew gently in amongst the tiny droplets, in a final embrace, and then moved away, no further words necessary between two friends who loved each other.

By now the draw to merge with the other parts floating in the air around it was totally irresistible to the little raindrop/mist and it felt a growing happiness within that caused great wonder.

As the individual droplets merged gently together, it found it could easily pick up on the experiences that each drop had had, as though it had been there with them, sharing it all, as it had shared the flower's life force. It learned about a water butt; a wet cat; fish; washing a car, being part of a reservoir, and getting 'drinked'... the little raindrop/mist's millions of particles smiled, remembering.

So many lives – all one. The sun was right: when you put it all together it added up, quite simply, to One Thing called **life**, and they were all a part of it – sharing, separate and yet all **one**.

And it *was* all about love.

The little raindrop/mist noticed that the more it merged now with the other droplets, the less it could see, and it was getting worse. Where was the forest below? Where was the beloved river? And then it realised: it was merging with the others to become part of a cloud once more and, in time, it would leave the cloud and fulfil its joint missions of giving sustenance to the earth below, and of accumulating more knowledge and understanding for the All.

This would happen many times, the little mist particles now knew, endlessly returning to the cloud, bringing back countless new experiences. There would be more answers to yet more questions, and the All would grow and grow.

Moving upwards to the base of the cloud now, the intrepid voyager eyed the sun, and winked. "I will fulfil my purpose, to the best of my ability, and make the All proud of me," it told the sun, without a word. The sun heard, and the little traveller joined the cloud. It couldn't see anything any more and it seemed not to be able to remember as well as it had done, but somehow it didn't matter as it settled into the white haze, in a state that you and I might call 'sleep'.

The day would come, in the fullness of time, when the little raindrop would disembark once more.

The drop of water had no knowledge of anything before it fell from the cloud. Nothing was, until the moment when it had suddenly *winked* into existence. Although it didn't yet know much, it *did* know this whooshy thing playing all around it, and it knew it was called 'Wind'.

"Wind?"

"Hello, little raindrop," breezed the wind lovingly, and it seemed to the raindrop, for one brief moment, that they had met before.

"Do I know you?"

"Yes. And no."

"Oh. I'm going to have to think about that, you know."

"I know."

...and the **All** smiled.

The End

orn in 1953, Wendy Garrison Todd enjoyed a secretarial career until 1986 when a back injury led her to alternative healing. She qualified as a Reflexologist in 1988 and set up her own private practice. Since then she has added Reiki, Counselling and, more recently, Life Coaching to her work. Wendy's spiritual interest began over 25 years ago, integrating spiritual learning into everyday living, and she now uses her knowledge to offer an holistic approach to her clients. It is from this background that *The Little Raindrop* was written: a book about life; a book of innocence and love; a book that reaches out and touches lives.

arah Zoutewelle-Morris (1949) is an artist and graphic designer. She has illustrated various adult and childrens books including *The Findhorn Family Cookbook, A Path without Tracks,* and *The Angel Colouring Book.* She lived in the Findhorn Foundation, a spiritual community in Scotland, for 6 years. Sarah has been expanding her art to include work in hospitals and nursing homes, including the leading of creativity workshops for healthcare professionals. She lives and works in the Netherlands with her woodworker husband Rende.

For further information about the Findhorn Foundation and the Findhorn Community, please contact:

Findhorn Foundation
The Visitors Centre
The Park, Findhorn IV36 3TZ, Scotland, UK
tel 01309 690311
enquiries@findhorn.org
www.findhorn.org

For a complete Findhorn Press catalogue, please contact:

Findhorn Press
305a The Park, Findhorn
Forres IV36 3TE
Scotland, UK
tel 01309 690582
fax 01309 690036
info@findhornpress.com
www.findhornpress.com